Little Pebble™

Celebrate Autumn
Pumpkins

by Erika L. Shores

raintree
a Capstone company — publishers

Raintree is an imprint of Capstone Global Library Limited, a company incorporated in England and Wales having its registered office at 7 Pilgrim Street, London, EC4V 6LB – Registered company number: 6695582

www.raintree.co.uk
myorders@raintree.co.uk

Text © Capstone Global Library Limited 2016
The moral rights of the proprietor have been asserted.

Editorial Credits
Edited by Mari Bolte and Erika Shores
designed by Cynthia Della-Rovere
picture research by Svetlana Zhurkin,
production by Morgan Walters

ISBN 978 1 4747 0298 0 (hardback)
19 18 17 16 15
10 9 8 7 6 5 4 3 2 1

ISBN 978 1 4747 0303 1 (paperback)
20 19 18 17 16 15
10 9 8 7 6 5 4 3 2 1

British Library Cataloguing in Publication Data
A full catalogue record for this book is available from the British Library.

Photo Credits
Dreamstime: Robin Van Olderen, 12, SandraRBarba, 6—7, Smellme, 16 (right); Newscom: ZUMA Press/Tony Crocetta, 26—27; Shutterstock: Aaron Amat, 27 (top), ala737, 13 (bottom), Alta Oosthuizen, 15 (top), 18, Ana Gram, 25, 29 (inset), bjogroet, 11 (top), Black Sheep Media (grass), throughout, Chantal de Bruijne (African landscape), back cover and throughout, creative, 10, e2dan, 13 (top), Eric Isselee, cover, back cover, 1, 4, 7 (top), 11 (bottom), 21 (top), 23 (top), 32, Gerrit_de_Vries, 14 (top), 17, Jez Bennett, 14 (bottom), John Michael Evan Potter, 9, Maggy Meyer, 28—29, MattiaATH, 8, Mogens Trolle, 15 (bottom), moizhusein, 20—21, 23, Moments by Mullineux, 5, Sean Stanton, 19, Serge Vero, 24, Stuart G. Porter, 22

Printed and Bound in China.

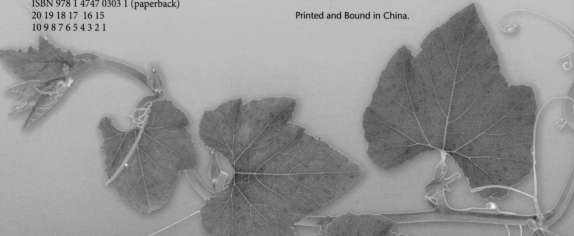

Contents

In autumn

The weather
becomes cooler.
It is autumn.

Look at the pumpkins!
They grow in a patch.

6

Pumpkins grow
on vines along
the ground.

vine

Grab pumpkins
by the stems.
Pile them into carts.

stem

Seeds

Cut into a pumpkin.

Take out the 200 seeds.

Seeds are sticky.

Save them.

Plant them in spring!

The sun shines.

Rain falls.

Watch the seeds sprout.

Vines grow.

Pumpkins get bigger.

Time to pick

the perfect one!

Glossary

patch small part or area

seed part that will grow into a new plant

sprout start to grow

stem part of a plant that connects the roots to the leaves

vine plant with a long thin stem that grows along the ground or up a fence

Read more

All About Seeds (All About Plants), Claire Throp (Raintree,2014)

Learning About Plants (The Natural World), Catherine Veitch (Raintree, 2012)

What Can You See in Autumn? (Seasons), Sian Smith (Raintree, 2014)

Websites

www.bbc.co.uk/gardening/digin/your_space/patch.shtml
Celebrate autumn by growing and harvesting fruit and vegetables in your garden or on your windowsill. Follow the BBC's step-by-step picture guide to help you get started.

www.naturedetectives.org.uk/autumn/
Download wildlife ID sheets, pick up some great autumn crafting ideas and collect recipes for some delicious autumn cooking projects on this website.

Index